Sim and Pim

By Sally Cowan

Sim sips.

Pim taps the sap.

Sim!

Pim!

Sim and Pim sat.

CHECKING FOR MEANING

1. What does Sim sip? *(Literal)*
2. Where do Sim and Pim sit? *(Literal)*
3. Why are Sim and Pim surprised? *(Inferential)*

EXTENDING VOCABULARY

taps	Look at the word *taps.* What is the base of this word? What has been added to the base? Can you think of another word that means the same as *taps*?
sap	Look at the word *sap*. What is sap? Where do you find it? What is Pim doing with the sap?
sat	Look at the word *sat*. Can you think of other words that rhyme with *sat*?

MOVING BEYOND THE TEXT

1. What special features do birds have?
2. Sim and Pim are honeyeaters. What other types of birds do you know?
3. What do you like to sip?
4. If you were a bird, where would you fly to?

SPEED SOUNDS

Mm	Ss	Aa	Pp	Ii	Tt

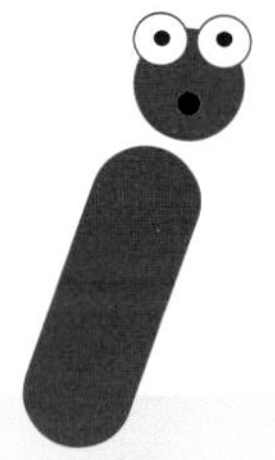

PRACTICE WORDS

sips

Sim

Pim

sap

taps

sat